Dedication

There are so many people who have played a vital part in our ministry and in these stories. We have some amazing prayer ministers: Dawn Leonard, Matt and Lilibeth Kindle, Rachel Mull, Andrew Mull, Deborah Cliver, and others who have been part of ministering to the people written about in these pages.

Father God deserves all the credit and glory. The Holy Spirit is responsible for every miracle and breakthrough. We often feel like we are spectators as God comes into the room and does what only He can do. We are somehow used to facilitate, in some small way, what God alone can do.

My beautiful and amazing wife has supported in the midst of so many adversities and plays a more significant role in the ministry of Operation Light Force than she gets credit for.

In the end, I also want to dedicate this book to those broken hearts that God has brought to us. You, Joy, and all the rest of you. God has used you to change our lives, forever. You are worth the time, the tears, and you are loved.

RESTORING JOY

RICHARD MULL

A JOURNEY TO
SPIRITUAL FREEDOM

Heal
THE BROKENHEARTED

THE SPIRIT OF THE LORD

is upon me, because he hath anointed me

to preach the gospel to the poor; he hath

sent me to heal the brokenhearted, to preach

deliverance to the captives, and recovering

of sight to the blind, to set at liberty

them that are bruised.

Luke 4:18

King James Version

RICHARD MULL
Restoring JOY

Table of Contents

Preface

FROM FREEDOM TO JOY!

I want to invite you into our world, the world of Operation Light Force (OLF) and Freedom Park. It is not a world that many get to see. When someone is healed of cancer or raised from the dead, it is easy to shout it from the mountain tops. I have participated in those types of miracles many times and have written about them. I believe such miracles are important and necessary and part of God's plan and kingdom on earth today.

For the last several years, we have been witnessing a different kind of miracle that is just as important. God has been sending us people who are in deep need of healing and freedom, but their stories are much harder to talk about. The types of brokenness and healing that we now see are not what I would have chosen to sign up for. We haven't even advertised for this type of ministry, but God keeps sending us hurting people who have survived horrendous traumas.

I will warn you in advance. There is a good reason we do not normally share the stories of what we typically see in our ministry. These are not the kinds of stories that give you warm fuzzies and good feelings. These are the kinds of stories that may cause you to cry, fill you with anger, or may even shock you as you grapple with the unthinkable evil that one human does to another. My hope is that these stories will also cause you to glorify God as you hear how lives have changed, light triumphed over darkness, and those who used to be slaves are now free. I hope that these stories will move you to compassion and action.

On a regular basis, God has been sending us people who have experienced severe and prolonged trauma as a significant part of their lives. The trauma may stem from an emotionally, verbally abusive parent, spiritual abuse in the home or in church. Another trauma that has impacted many is the death of family members and friends, especially if that loss occurred during childhood. Those are real and devastating traumas and have lasting impact in a person's life. But we also regularly deal with things that are unbelievable, unimaginable, and hard to stomach.

Some of the people whom God sends to us for ministry have been diagnosed with various disorders. We see Dissociative Identity Disorder or DID, formerly called Multiple Personality Disorder, on a regular basis. The Mayo Clinic describes this as the presence of two or more distinct personality identities, often with each having a unique name, history, and characteristics. It usually results from trauma as a way of avoiding bad memories. The American Medical Association says it is incurable.

With God, all things are possible. God is an amazing healer, and He deserves all the glory for those who have been healed. What is impossible with man is not hard for God.

God knows every day of everyone's life. He cares about every trauma and can heal people from their traumas. It is amazing to watch what God does with the hearts and lives of people who have experienced the unimaginable.

The stories in this book are real and paint a small picture of what God is doing in the lives of people whom He loves.

I have permission to write about the life of everyone whose stories are contained in this book. I have changed the names and been vague enough that most who are not intimately familiar with their stories won't be able to guess who I'm writing about.

These are amazing people, serving in churches, living relatively normal lives. Some are in ministry, some are in the workforce, and some are housewives. But all are still damaged and impacted by the traumas they endured for much of their lives. They all have a testimony of God's bringing them to a place of freedom, wholeness and victory. All of them are still on a journey for more freedom, more wholeness and more victory. All of them have a heart to see others, like themselves, find the help and healing they have experienced.

As you read these stories, many of you will be tempted to question the validity of what I write. What God has allowed us to deal with in ministry is often the stuff of movies and what many think are fictional Hollywood stories. The things we hear day in and day out deal with groups like the CIA, Special Forces, NASA, Hollywood, biker gangs, KKK, secret societies, real life human trafficking, mind-control programming and more.

Some of you may be wanting to stop already, because you don't want to accept that any of this could be real. I completely understand. Most of my life I didn't want to believe that what I now see on a daily basis was real. I still would greatly prefer a world where everything that I write about is a pretend story, fantasy or make believe.

I promise you this: it's real, and what I write is all true. Everyone whom I have included in these stories has verified the details that I have written. This is a PG book that is made up of XXX horror stories. I am telling you a lot without telling you much. For each of these individuals, you are only reading a small portion of their history. A short glimpse into their life. I will spare you the gory details, as they can be disturbing and are not necessary for you to see how God has moved in each person's life to set them free from slavery.

God wants His church—you, me, all of us—to be able to respond to the global crisis that is at hand. Just doing church services will not be enough to heal these broken hearts and lives.

My primary goal in writing this is to obey God. He has been telling me to expose the darkness and prepare His church for ministering and bringing healing to the massive number of people whom He is delivering from the grips of abuse, trauma, pedophilia, trafficking and mind-control.

I know that anyone who reads this will be impacted and forced to respond. One response is to not read. Another is to close your eyes and pretend none of it is real and go on living in whatever reality you want to. But most believers will want to know what they can do. You want to make a difference.

Let me encourage you. It will be ok to cry, to feel sad, to feel angry. God has felt everything you will feel and exponentially more. He cares more. He feels more. He loves more. These things break His heart.

I won't hold it against you if you struggle to believe whether some of what I write is true. But please don't be too quick to dismiss these stories. Ask the Holy Spirit to confirm to you if these stories merely come from overactive imaginations. I know that some people think all these types of memories are manmade. If you could ask the women and men we minister to, they would tell you that nothing we did created these memories. They already struggled with these memories when they came for ministry. Many had opened up to counselors only to be told they didn't know how to help, or that their memories couldn't be real, or that they needed drugs because they were crazy.

Again, if you met these people, you would not be able to look at them and tell that anything is wrong in their lives. They could be your best friend and have become good at keeping their secrets. Who would believe them anyway? Many tried to tell someone and found that the person they confided in, perhaps a family member, only added to their abuse. They have many times sworn never to trust anyone again.

I have included scriptures throughout this book that demonstrate God's heart for the broken hearted. I teach two courses on Healing the Broken Hearted in our online university and have recorded conferences on this subject. If you want a more in-depth study about what the Bible has to say about God's heart towards the broken hearted, I invite you to investigate these resources. However, this book is not written to be a teaching on that subject, it is meant to glorify God in telling what he does for the broken hearted. The stories matter because they reflect how far the enemy will go to destroy someone's soul, and how much greater God's power is to redeem a soul. It would be worth your time to just thumb through the pages and see God's heart and what the Word says about all of this. Jesus lists healing the broken hearted as one of the marks of his ministry in Luke 4:18.

In the last chapter, I hope to spell out more clearly what you can do in response. I encourage you not to let this be a quick read that you try to ignore or forget. At least be willing to ask God one question, and don't be afraid of what God may say to you. Here is the question: "God, what do you want me to do about what *Restoring Joy* is revealing to me?"

IF MY PEOPLE,

who are called by My name will
humble themselves, and pray and
seek My face, and turn from their
wicked ways, then I will hear
from heaven, and will forgive
their sin and heal their land.

2 CHRONICLES 7:14
New King James Version

By: *Jeffrey Damm*

A BROTHER IN CHRIST AND DEAR FRIEND OF RICHARD

BY MOST NOVEL STANDARDS, the 'foreword' is typically written by some world renowned authority figure that studies and works in the same field of the book's topic to establish a sense of ethos or credibility with the reader. In this particular case, this person would need to have a pedigree in spiritual and psychological behavior coupled with tribal knowledge into the world of human trafficking, broken hearted souls and satanic ritual behaviors. This is *not* the case. I am modestly, Jeffrey Damm, a brother in Christ and dear friend to Richard Mull. We have been together on this Christ-centric mission called, Operation Light Force, since it's inception circa 1999ish. Over 21+ years ago, what started as a professional relationship grew into a lasting friendship between two men of God. Well, Richard more so with his walk with Christ than me, but that's an entirely different book.

Recently, Richard and I have been drawn even closer together by God's divine orchestration through *His* vision of Freedom Park. It all started several years ago as Richard's concept of a sanctuary for individuals, couples and families to live in affordable healing style housing while they focus on their physical, spiritual and emotional healing through ministry. In 2020, it was estimated that there were 40.3 million victims of human trafficking globally. The state of Florida was ranked as having the third-highest human trafficking rate in 2019. But these are not just numbers, they represent boys and girls, men and women who are alive and trapped in a global crisis promoting slavery.

In early 2021, my beautiful wife Jaimee and I became the first on-sight residence of Freedom Park. Richard provided us with an RV on OLF property so we can focus solely on our healing. This was historic—Freedom Park had begun! We even laughed on certain days that we were TEAM ALPHA. We smiled but knew a great journey had begun.

We learned so much from the talented staff about broken souls, soul ties, and spiritual healing. After some time in healing sessions the inevitable happened—TRUE SUBMISSION that ultimately led to SALVATION. You see, when the children of God do what is right and just, we benefit from God's true healing power. FREEDOM begins with submission to God's authority. It sets order and direction in our everyday lives for those found in Christ. And what is to follow is unimaginable healing and blessing for those who are obedient.

Our perfect teacher in this area of submission to authority is Jesus himself. We learn, throughout his 33 years on Earth, including the three years of ministry that led up to Christ's death and resurrection, he displayed total submission to God's authority. It was out of this submission to authority and love that we were redeemed from the curse of sin.

It is never enough to be a "good person." Submitting to God, repentance, acceptance of Christ as Lord and savior, and allowing his authority to reign in our lives is required. When you and I have learned how to respect the authority of God, we will be in a position to do the same here on Earth.

This was BIG for Jaimee and myself!

Titus 2:11-14 For the grace of God has appeared, bringing salvation to all people. It trains us to reject godless ways and worldly desires and to live self-controlled, upright, and godly lives in the present age, as we wait for the happy fulfillment of our hope in the glorious appearing of our great God and Savior, Jesus Christ.

Sadly, we realized we were facing eternal judgment and in our self-seeking pride I could not see it. But eventually God disciplined us, allowed repentance, and gave us his loving mercy. When you have been humbled and raised up by The Sovereign God you must begin to speak more of Him rather than ourselves.

1 PETER 4 So, since Christ suffered in the flesh, you also arm yourselves with the same attitude, because the one who has suffered in the flesh has finished with sin, in that he spends the rest of his time on earth concerned about the will of God and not human desires.

For the time that has passed was sufficient for you to do what the non-Christians desire. You lived then in debauchery, evil desires, drunkenness, carousing, drinking bouts, and idolatries. Guilty as charged!!

We learned a new life individually!

EPHESIANS 2 And although you were dead in your transgressions and sins, in which you formerly lived according to this world's present path, according to the ruler of the kingdom of the air, the ruler of the spirit that is now energizing the sons of disobedience, among whom all of us also formerly lived out our lives in the cravings of our flesh, indulging the desires of the flesh and the mind, and were by nature children of wrath even as the rest.

...and finally self-purification!

2 COR 7:1 Therefore, since we have these promises let us cleanse ourselves from everything that could defile the body and the spirit, and thus accomplish holiness out of reverence for God.

Thank you Richard Mull and the Freedom Park staff for being dear friends and an instrumental part of our salvation.

Encountering Joy

I got a call one day from a woman whom we had ministered to years ago. She had a friend, Joy (not her real name), who wanted to get out of the occult, away from a life of darkness, drugs, prostitution, the slavery of the occult and human trafficking. And she wanted to follow Jesus.

The person who had made this call had at one time been a leader in the occult at a very high level. She had been a trained assassin and was at one time being groomed to program others as well. Now she is a woman of God, married to a godly man and has been serving in a women's ministry and speaking in prisons.

Until recently we were among the only people who knew her story because no one would have believed it. Now, she was calling me to tell me about her friend Joy. She asked if Freedom Park was ready to take her in. It was May, and we had just failed to reach the mark we needed to buy the properties adjacent to ours. It had seemed that Freedom Park was still a future vision, but God was telling us to get creative, that NOW was the time. NOW was the hour, with or without the money or the buildings.

Freedom Park was just a vision. It was a vision without property or buildings or staff, but it was already starting to function. We had a couple living on site who had both lived through serious abuse. They needed ministry after they had become homeless and battled with addictions. They were experiencing some freedom and growing in the Lord, but it stretched our team to be dealing with the issues that this couple were facing. Now we had a request for another resident for our unformed Freedom Park.

I brought Joy's situation and circumstances up to our team, who tend to roll their eyes a lot when God brings these kinds of things our way. They must have been wondering, "What is Richard getting us into now?" As for me, I was wondering, "What is God getting us into now?" I know of no other program that is equipped to both handle and house people who have lived through satanic ritual abuse and human trafficking.

This is the stuff that movies are made about, and we treat it like fantasy, like fiction. IT IS REAL! It is dark! It is way more prevalent than we want to believe, accept, or imagine.

For some of you, the term "satanic ritual abuse" (SRA) may be a new phrase. The sad truth is, there are many different forms of satanic cult groups in our nation. A part of this world always involves ceremonies where children, women, and men are used in sexual and trauma rituals. We honestly deal with this on a weekly or daily basis. Most of the stories in this book involve some form of SRA activity.

As I mentioned, we didn't have land or a place, just a vision and a fledgling start. It is so important to God that people like Joy have a place to turn to that He connects them to us. We don't have to search for them.

We purchased a second fifth-wheel trailer at a fraction of its true value.

And Freedom Park Beta was in place. Plans were made to bring Joy across the US to Operation Light Force. She had no money, a bag full of clothes, some cigarettes and little else. So, Joy came to OLF and Freedom Park.

Every day, in every ministry session, I wanted to cry. I wanted to expel the contents of my previous meal. I wanted to adopt this girl. She has given me permission to tell her story, which I plan to do more fully, if God wills, at some point. The hardest part of telling it is trying to make anything palatable enough for you to stomach.

How do you write such a horrible story into a PG-rating that adequately helps people know what is really going on in our world today? The stories of things done to her, said to her, endured by her for 30-plus years of her life are unimaginable. I have worked in this field of ministry for over 20 years, and it was still so disturbing. I didn't hear anything that I hadn't heard before, but it was still profoundly heart-wrenching.

Let me try to paint a picture that tells a lot without getting into details. It begins with a "father" telling you that you are special and created for one purpose—namely, to serve the deviant desires of evil people. It is a tale of drugs given to create addictions and the use of those drugs for the purpose of manipulating, controlling, and enslaving you. The drugs are not taken in defiance of the law, but in innocent obedience by a child. It is a tale of gross perversions made to seem normal and ordinary. It is the story of police, federal agents, government officials, all operating together to protect each other and cash in on darkness. When many of the abusers are religious leaders, governmental leaders, family members and others in leadership positions, where can you turn? Who can be trusted? It is a tale of satanic rituals, trafficking, and horrors of the real-life hunting of human beings for sport and pleasure.

This is the stuff that movies are made about, and we treat it like fantasy, like fiction. IT IS REAL! It is dark! It is way more prevalent than we want to believe, accept, or imagine.

Ministering to Joy was a delight, as she ate up freedom like a famished traveler would engulf a meal. She would read and meditate on God's Word. She loved the book of Hosea and how God redeemed a harlot. She saw herself as she read through Israel's pursuit of God and then relapse toward evil. She wanted to follow Jesus with all her heart and rescue other girls.

I have a tendency to fall in love with the people God sends to us for ministry. I mean that in the purest way, no matter what it sounds like. They get in my heart, and I care about them and for them. Joy definitely got to my heart. If I could, I would adopt her.

When Joy in a season of weakness turned back to her former ways of making money and allowed other addictions to take her back into the prisons she had left behind, it was devastating. As a ministry we did not have the personnel in place to provide the kind of oversight and care that Joy needed. It was Joy who came to us and confessed what she had done. We responded with love and grace. We wanted to work through these things and help her.

At the same time all this was transpiring, I had several team members step down, my wife was facing surgery, and we could not find anyone to step up. We knew we were dealing with programmed addictions that would not go away easily. We had to come to the brutal conclusion that we were not at this time able to respond to all that was needed to continue to minister to Joy. Caring for her would take more human resources than we had available. We also needed a different living situation where there would be more accountability and oversight.

All of us believe that the outcome would have been different if we had all those things in place.

Joy had never experienced the ability to trust anyone in her world. Every one of her family and friendships were involved in darkness. At one time, Joy had even moved into a home for victims of human trafficking, only to find out that Satanists were running the home and she was enslaved in a place she had turned to for freedom. We tried to find other places to send her. Two temporary homes opened up, but with her history, she was not willing to trust another place.

Joy had to leave us. But she wants to come back, and we want to receive her back. We want to restore Joy. We want to teach transgressors the ways of the Lord, so that sinners will turn back to the Lord, as it says in Psalm 51.

I told Joy that if we could raise the funds and hire the staff, we needed that I would bring her back. Right now, the only world she knows is the one she left behind to come to OLF. I wept for days and have lost a lot of sleep praying for Joy. I want to help settle Joy in a place where she is loved. A place where she can find freedom and a place where she can help us start to rescue a multitude of other Joys.

CREATE IN ME A PURE HEART,

O God, and renew a steadfast spirit within

me. Do not cast me from your presence or

take your Holy Spirit from me. Restore to

me the joy of your salvation and grant me

a willing spirit, to sustain me. Then I will

teach transgressors your ways, so that

sinners will turn back to you.

PSALM 51:10-13

Imagine believing for your entire life that you grew up in a good Christian home, only to find out that you and your family have been involved in a global pedophile ring. It didn't make too much sense when we first met Kelly (not her real name). She had several children and had laid down a firm rule that her parents were not allowed to see her children, their own grandchildren. She had worked hard to convince her husband that it was not safe. That was no easy task, since her parents had been so generous and loving over the years. Her parents served in a ministry that rescued children from human trafficking. They were generous people and full of life. They had given much to Kelly and her husband and were serious about their desire to help with the grandchildren.

As we began a week of ministry and she shared more of her story, those concerns gained a little bit of credibility. Then as more and more memories surfaced, we both began to put the pieces together to understand why her concerns regarding her family were so well founded.

Funding for her parents' ministry came not from traditional missionary support but from the military-industrial complex (companies that profit from the military and the defense industry). The particular organization they were associated with was also known to have a historically high-level connection to satanism and the occult.

The missionary children in her parents' ministry were affiliated with a NATO military base and all the kids went to school there. It was the same place that Kelly had gone to school. As she began to recall things that had happened during her school years and in her own subsequent military service, we all came to realize that she had been through extensive MKUltra mind control training.

We have dealt with many clients who have been through various aspects of this evil and dark training that the US and foreign governments and military groups have partaken of all around the world. The names change and the types of training become more sophisticated, but we will use the term mind control programming throughout this book to summarize a lot of unbelievable, demonically inspired atrocities that are being used upon so many children and adults in so many arenas today.

We have ministered to people from all walks of life and from many countries around the globe who have experienced these forms of mind control and abuse. Some experienced it in Hollywood, some on military bases, some by therapists, some by people in the government system or legal system. It appears that the abuse is widespread.

It was easy to put the pieces of the puzzle together that made up Kelly's story. It was easy to figure out what her family members were really up to when you looked at all the pieces. My staff member and I were seeing all the pieces, and it was very disturbing. I asked Kelly at one point, "Do you know what your parents were doing?" She was looking at all the evidence that she had set before us as if for the very first time. She looked visibly disturbed. I would not have told her what she said. I would not have made an accusation despite overwhelming evidence.

Kelly said, "My parents are part of a global pedophile ring." To protect her I won't give you all of the evidence, but I was doing my internet searches while she was telling the stories to confirm things. Details lined up on every point. It connected well known Satanists, satanic organizations, the military industrial complex, NATO, and governmental leaders to a very large front organization that looked like a Christian ministry to rescue victims of human trafficking. In reality, it was just false external packaging to hide the darkness behind the facade.

We have ministered to people from all walks of life and from many countries around the globe who have experienced these forms of mind control and abuse.

Kelly had become a Spirit-filled woman of God and a serious student of God's Word. She had been to secular therapists, military counselors and therapists, and various Christian healing and deliverance ministries. It was hard to swallow, but suddenly so many things made more sense in her life. The years of darkness and turning from God, all kinds of sexual issues and reactions from doctors over the years when she would be examined. They knew she had been seriously sexually abused, while she had no memories of it. Not only was it sexual abuse, but it was also demonically inspired, programmed sexual abuse.

Repeatedly we are ministering to people who, like Kelly, grew up in a home that outwardly had a facade of Christianity, but behind the scenes horrific and unimaginable evil was taking place. For some it is a Catholic facade where priests are actively involved in both pedophilia as well as satanic rituals. But we have ministered to individuals from almost every mainline denomination who suffered these atrocities while also going through all the motions of church life. Many times their family members have even been involved in leadership at these churches. This really makes it hard to separate out the real Jesus and real Christianity from the false. This mixture of religion and darkness is done intentionally to bring confusion about God, His power, His love and so much more. It takes a miracle of God to heal this kind of trauma and the confusion created by deceptively tying God into the trauma. But God is doing that! He is healing and setting people free and restoring people like Kelly.

God worked miraculously to bring Kelly to a place of not only freedom, but of authority and power and a desire to help others find the freedom she now enjoys. Her body and soul still carry the scars. But the Light of God's love and His healing power have brought not only freedom but fullness of His joy.

THE SACRIFICES OF GOD

are a broken spirit; a broken and contrite

heart, O God, you will not despise.

PSALM 51:17 (ESV)

Homeschool Mom

CHAPTER 3

When Rosy came for ministry, she looked like the typical homeschool mom, if there is a typical. She had poured her life into her kids and into her marriage for most of her life and sought to serve God and raise her family in the church. Hearing God's voice was a challenge, her marriage was in shambles, and she had been hurt so many times by the institutional churches where she had sought to serve and give 100% of herself toward their success. Abandonment, rejection, and spiritual abuse both at home and in the church had created walls of self-preservation. It required much time to break through these defenses and earn her trust.

Nothing about her story was unfamiliar at the beginning. It seems like everyone has had a host of familiar traumas. Tragedy has struck everyone at some point, but for some it has become a more regular part of life. That was the case for Rosy. The abuse she experienced from the church and trusted spiritual leaders and other "Christian" friends of the family left major scars and fearful trauma to her soul.

Why had these things taken place? What was wrong with her? These were the questions that plagued her every day. She figured that it was her fault. She didn't want to make another mistake, get too close, let someone else down and have them abandon her as well. You can imagine the vicious cycle of wanting to hide from relationships and at the same time having the desire and need to conform and perform for acceptance and belonging.

Imagine being experimented on sexually, physically, mentally and emotionally to the breaking point just like the men who sign up for the special forces and you never even signed up for the training.

Little did she know that she and her own children had experienced severe and prolonged abuse at the hands of people of whom, in their conscious memories, they had mostly fond memories. She had grown up, like many others, with multiple dads. Death, divorce and outright rejection by each of the different males who occupied that position for periods of her life left gaping wounds in her heart. The concept of God as Father was not too hard to grasp at an intellectual level, but experience made it nearly impossible to truly comprehend or experience the joys of such a relationship.

There was only one of the men who occupied the role of father in her life who she felt like cared about her. She had been young, but this military man had spent time with her. He had played with her, talked and listened to her, and hugged and comforted her. The memories she had of him made her think that at least one father had loved her and cared for her.

When God began to reveal her past to her and heal trauma after trauma, so beautifully, tenderly and powerfully, it was surprising to all of us when God began to show Rosy the truth about this father. He had been taking her every day to a secret military school that was designed to program her in unbelievable and unimaginable ways. When things like this come up in ministry, we are often led to research to find out if there is anything to validate what a person begins to share as they recover traumatic memories. A very high percentage of the time, with minimal research, we can find things to substantiate the memories a person begins to recover.

In Rosy's case there were specific details that she recalled that seemed rather far-fetched. But within minutes of research, we had proof of details that she could not have known about as a civilian, or even the child of someone in the military. She had been in underground military installations whose existence had been denied by our military till more recently. This, and other declassified government documents outlining experimental training programs for children, took her stories from the overactive imagination of a child to the realm of a real-life survivor of governmental corruption at a national level.

The horrors that Rosy, and Kelly from the last chapter, and millions of others like them around the world have been forced to endure are hard to comprehend. Imagine as a child having to decide which person in your classroom gets shocked electrically, or yourself. Imagine having to spy on other kids to make sure they don't run away from the next horrific exercise or experiment, just like a gestapo guard, because if you don't maintain order and keep the others in line something worse will await all of you. Imagine being experimented on sexually, physically, mentally and emotionally to the breaking point just like the men who sign up for the special forces and you never even signed up for the training.

The things done to children like Rosy and so many others we meet, awaken sexuality and twist and pervert it at a young age. As these children grow older, they act out sexually in very self-destructive ways and are filled with shame. They grow up believing there is something horribly wrong with themselves. They often struggle with sexual thoughts, fantasies, masturbation, and experimentation.

Imagine all the drugs you would have to take so that these memories would never come back to haunt you. Now imagine as an adult thinking you are crazy because the walls that have kept those memories locked away are starting to crumble and spill over into real life. What happens when you start to tell your pastor, church small group, or friends? What happens when you tell most counselors who have never heard of or believed in any of this? You are likely sent to a psychiatrist, told you are crazy, and given more medications.

Many of the people who come to us for ministry have become Christians and are active in their churches and communities. They have often had these secret and quiet struggles throughout their lives and have learned to manage them, keeping them hidden to varying degrees. They have a ton of moral failures that cause them to question their own worth and their salvation. These struggles and failures have landed them in counselors' offices, therapists' offices, and pastors' offices for most of their lives.

It is God's grace that destroys that wall around the locked closets of their mind, heart and soul. It is God's mercy that allows them to get just a glimpse of the atrocities they were forced to endure so that He can begin to heal the damage done to them in the past. So that they can walk forward free from the demonic and diabolical programming forced on them.

In ministry session after session God shows up and speaks to the broken places with love and tenderness. He rescues these precious souls again and again and proves His love to them to restore hope, to give them the capacity to trust again, to really love Him and others.

Some of the people God sends to us never break through the trust barrier. They have sworn to never trust anyone, and nothing we say or do or God says or does overcomes that vow. Most find a love they never could have imagined, healing from the traumas and scars, freedom from the stronghold that held them captive, and family that cares. Some go on to minister to others and begin to have more viable and lasting relationships with God and with others than they ever dreamed possible.

Recently, I asked Rosy a question. "When you look back on the ministry that you have received at OLF, what stands out as having impacted you the most?" Written below is her response.

"There is not just one breakthrough moment that stands out above all the others; there are many breakthrough moments that happened in the healing process. As I write, so many sessions and encounters with Jesus are going through my head. I will share with you just a few:

"As you read in Richard's synopsis of my story, abandonment by my dad and abuse by my stepdad left me with a big black hole of longing to be loved by a dad but an inability to connect with Father God. Even though I knew with my head that the Bible says that God loves me, my heart could never get rid of the doubts and fears that God would reject and abandon me. When I was in desperate need

He rescues these precious souls again and again and proves His love to them to restore hope, to give them the capacity to trust again, to really love Him and others.

and would cry out to Him, I didn't believe that He would come. Because of this, I would have times of absolute hopelessness and despair where I felt all alone and I was sure that God had abandoned me.

"Then I started receiving ministry at OLF: Richard stood in the gap and repented for everything that I experienced from fathers. He told me about the Father's love. He sang of the Father's love and then He spoke a father's blessing over me. I felt Daddy God's love! It was amazing and life changing. It was the beginning of me being able to believe with my head and my heart that Daddy God loves me, that He will never abandon me!

"I have a big brother who was my hero when I was young. He was the consistent male in my life. I felt safe when he was near. When I was around nine years old, he abandoned me too. This had devastating results on the way I saw myself—something must be wrong with me that everyone leaves. It had devastating results on the way I saw Jesus—big brothers will abandon me. It added to my daddy wounds, because he was a father figure. When Richard stood in the gap as a big brother, I cried and cried and cried. Richard became a bridge to God. I started to believe that if this man that was standing in front of me knew all these things about me and still accepted me, then maybe God did too.

"Another time, I was asking God about a memory that I had during a session. The memory was painful, and I was full of shame. I saw a vision of myself during the memory. This time Jesus was there looking on. I had so much shame that I was sure that Jesus would be disappointed and disgusted with me. But He wasn't. He cried as He saw what I was doing to myself. He cried as I experienced pain and shame. He didn't look at me with disgust and disappointment. He didn't turn his back on me. He shared my pain. He comforted me. I am not a disappointment to Him!

"Another poignant memory is the vision I had of myself as a child in a filthy dress. Jesus let me take a bubble bath, and then He gave me a beautiful princess dress. I felt so clean and pretty. I twirled around in the dress. Jesus continued to take all my shame away.

"In other sessions, Jesus spoke to me about my life. He talked to me about resting sometimes, about not needing to perform for others. He showed me that it's okay to take time to play. He told me how He delights in me. He spoke to me about my fears and taught me how to trust Him.

"Through these encounters with God and many others like them, I learned with my head and my heart how much Daddy God loves me. I now know He is not disappointed in me. I know that He loves me! I can hear His voice. I have peace and joy. I have more confidence. I know that I have value—I'm not trash and I don't deserve to be given trash or treated like trash. I've learned about God's kingdom and that I'm an heir in that kingdom. I've learned that I have authority in Jesus and that I don't have to just let the enemy beat me up or beat up those I love.

"I don't hate myself anymore, so I'm able to love God, love me, and love others more effectively. I now share with others what God has done in me, and I help them find the healing, freedom, and love that I've found."

AND THE VERY GOD OF PEACE

sanctify you wholly; and [I pray God]

your whole spirit and soul and body be

preserved blameless unto the coming of

our Lord Jesus Christ.

1 THESSALONIANS 5:23

TRAINED TO BE

An Assassin

CHAPTER 4

In 2013, God made Dillion Killingsworth (the name she chose for herself) a promise. He told her that he would remove the tares that were put in her when she was yet in her mother's womb and that He would make her whole.

When Dillion was a little girl she could hear God, but she also had a lot of darkness in her world. The darkness in her could not comprehend God nor what God was speaking to her at that time, but she wouldn't forget that voice.

Dillion's childhood was subject to the entrapments of pain, rejection, regret, disappointment, rage, SRA (satanic ritual abuse), and severe brainwashing that had sunk its roots into the very core of who she thought she was. Dillion had no identity and no peace. During this period, the Lord was continuing a good work in her, but time and space had not yet revealed the promises God made to her as a little girl.

The types and the severity of the traumas she had endured as an infant were so severe and hard for anyone to believe, much less imagine. It would likely disturb your sleep to hear about the things she was forced to endure by her own mother and the satanic culture she was involved in. This led to a lifetime of bad choices and further trauma.

Unlike many similar stories, Dillion was rescued at a fairly young age and adopted by a godly Christian family. That family had no idea what they had signed on for. They continuously loved Dillion even though she made it difficult, if not impossible sometimes. No one understood the forces behind all that was happening. The darkness always seemed to be calling Dillion back. In her late teens and early 20's she began to pursue the things of darkness and quickly found herself in the midst of a family of organized crime and serial killers. That became her world.

In her own words, "God's righteous right hand reached down and caused divine intervention to miraculously manifest in my life."

Dillion ended up marrying into a family that on the outside looked like they had it all together, but underneath that facade was a world of darkness and evil and occult. Her husband was high up in the Masonic order and would beat her mercilessly on a daily basis. All of this was producing a rage that the occult world knew how to exploit. She was being groomed to hate. When they finally took her children from her something broke inside. She began to plot revenge and was trained by several other groups how to do what they had been grooming her to do. Take lives. For Dillion, religion played a big part of that programming. She believed that everything she was doing was righteous anger and that she was part of David's army.

She is writing an amazing and compelling account of her journey in a brand new book. Details coming soon! It is a story of horrific abuse, mind control, satanism, and assassin training. More importantly, it is a story of incredible redemption, salvation and great authority and freedom. That is where our stories and life journeys intersect.

In April of 2018, after years of seeking, searching, rehab and counseling, Dillion began to cry out to God and remind Him of the promise He had made to her. She knew that something hidden deeply within herself remained untouched by His power. There was a fortified separation between her spirit, soul, and body. Although she was surrounded by mighty people of God on a daily basis who were teaching, guiding, loving, and praying for her, these walls could not be penetrated.

In her desperation, she found herself googling her "symptoms" on her phone. Her search pulled up an article with the heading, "Broken Soul Ministry." She was expecting medical journals to pop up with descriptions about her psychological depravity and incurable state of mind. But God had other plans.

In her own words, "God's righteous right hand reached down and caused divine intervention to miraculously manifest in my life." As she read the broken soul article found on the Operation Light Force website, she could sense an immediate number sequence unlocking the gate to the fortified city of her heart, soul, and body. Before she was even able to speak to anyone from the Operation Light Force team, she began asking Jesus to be her savior from different places inside of herself. It was like all the broken parts of her heart wanted to be one whole heart that followed Jesus. This provoked hope and faith to rise up in her, and the promise the Lord made to her in 2013 began to come alive.

A few months later, she had her first session with me and my team. She testifies that from the first session and in all that followed, those ministering to her would speak what God had been speaking to her already—scripture, prophetic words, even songs that Holy Spirit had been using to minister to her. Parts of her soul that had been trapped in darkness and unbelief received the love of Christ, salvation, and His resurrection power. In her own words, "with the gentleness of a summer breeze, the Lord uses Richard and his team to do the work of making me WHOLE! I am amazed at the dramatic results that I experience during each strategic session."

The healing that comes when her soul is restored to the Lord is the picture I want to paint. This has been an amazing, life-transforming work of Almighty God. Dillion is a new creation. She is more than alive and much more than a survivor. She has learned to thrive and is ready to pull others out of her former world and heal them.

Imagine, if you will, a tar pit. In this bottomless tar pit are traumas such as SRA (satanic ritual abuse), abandonment, severe physical and verbal abuse, emotional neglect, addictions, secret societies, confusion, hate, hopelessness, false doctrines, and torment. Worst of all, imagine the shame of inflicting some of these same traumas on her own family, her own children, and others in her path, all being trapped in this vortex of time with no oxygen and no light.

This was where Dillion saw herself. Her body, soul, and heart were being tortured. She believed they were lost. She felt like her soul was blind, dumb and deaf.

She claims that, "Operation Light Force, cloaked in a mantle of revelation knowledge and grace, used their weapons of warfare to save me from myself." To Him be all glory, honor and praise!

Now, Dillion is out of that tar pit and can see color. She breathes the very breath of God. She is now free to love, to live, believe in "good", and to believe in herself.

Dillion wrote this!

"I drink from the crystal sea and I eat from the Tree of Life (which, I must say, the fruit is heavenly!) I feel the sun kiss my skin and I take my time everyday anticipating what God has planned for me. I walk in expectation with my head held high, as the Lion of the Tribe of Judah roars within my heart, causing my heart to beat for what makes His beat. Jesus has restored back to me my strength and dignity.

"I am and will be eternally grateful to Richard Mull and his team at Operation Light Force for answering the call of the Commander of the army of the Lord. I hope to one day join their ranks and in turn, give to others what has been given to me."

It has been a privilege to be part of Dillion's ongoing journey. You will definitely want to get a copy of her book when it is released and read a more in-depth version of her story. I've gotten a sneak peak and it is a real page turner from the first paragraph. I expect that if the Lord tarries and God wills, her book will be a movie one day.

Truthfully, every one of the stories in this book deserves to be told, and what God has done is so remarkable. I count it a privilege every day to serve a great King who heals and sets captives free. He loves the brokenhearted and comes to rescue them.

Church Trauma

CHAPTER 5

Sarah was a young mom who came to the office one day because her marriage was in shambles. She needed help. She was exhausted emotionally, physically, spiritually, and she had no idea why she was suffering from daily panic attacks. She grew up in a Christian home, was homeschooled, was raising her kids in the church, and she had no idea how her life had gotten so out of control.

When she started to share her story, it didn't make sense to her or to anyone else how she got to where she was or why she faced some of her struggles until she started to recover memories. At first there were memories of a close family friend molesting her repeatedly over the span of many years. Then there were the memories of things that had actually happened while at church.

She would ride to church with her parents and siblings. Her parents would drop her off at the children's church. She and some of the other children were taken to another room where unspeakable things were done to them. Satanic rituals were performed, and the children were forced to participate in many perverted practices. This happened while her parents were in another part of the church worshipping God. Can you imagine the horror she felt as she remembered and relived these events? Now she understood the unexplainable fears she had felt as she took her kids and dropped them off at school or church. Somewhere inside she was always wondering if the things that happened to her could be happening to them.

Suddenly, so many things in her life made sense: the weird reactions she had experienced to her husband on her honeymoon, her acceptance of the horrible ways her husband treated her, the irrational phobias and fears she had, the crazy nightmares, the sexual temptations; it all made sense now.

So many women who have been through the kinds of things Sarah went through grow up thinking they were evil from birth. Even as little girls they have sexual awareness and ungodly sexual thoughts. When abuse happened in the church, then the temptations and thoughts will often come while they are at church and they don't know why. All they can think is that they are purely evil.

I wish I could tell you that Sarah's story is rare or unusual, but I can't. Client after client comes to us and tells us story after story of being molested at church or at school by a teacher, pastor, or Boy Scout leader. The very people that we teach our children to trust are the ones who perform unspeakable evils upon them. Because of the numerous scandals that have been exposed, many people think of this as something that only happens in the Catholic Church. But Sarah's story happened in an Assembly of God church. We've heard these stories from Baptist churches, Pentecostal churches, Church of Christ, Methodist, etc. We have dealt with people who were molested by mega-church pastors who are well known.

There are so many hurting adults, so many hurting teens, so many hurting children who need to have an encounter with the real Jesus. They need to know that God never sanctioned these things that have been done to them. The things that caused their silence for so long were the messages(lies) that they were taught- that what they were experiencing is God's plan or that they are special and chosen by God for these encounters.

Many things that we hear fill us with righteous anger. Few things give me greater anger, related to abuse, than does abuse that is in God's name. Part of satan's strategy and design for this kind of abuse is to make it impossible for a person to come to experience God's love and healing through Jesus.

The very people that we teach our children to trust are the ones who perform unspeakable evils upon them. Because of the numerous scandals that have been exposed, many people think of this as something that only happens in the Catholic Church.

As I write, my anger just turned to laughter. It is with great joy that I testify that Sarah and many others like her have come to encounter the real Jesus and His love and to know the Father's love, in spite of satan's evil deeds.

The men and women, like Sarah, who have been through this kind of abuse need to meet the real heavenly Father who will love them, heal them, and set them free from the internal prisons that these horrendous experiences have created. Many of them need a safe place to live, a place where they can receive care and love as they heal from their wounds and receive God's unconditional love.

God loves the broken-hearted, and He binds up their wounds. He is close to the broken-hearted. He hears their cries and dries their tears.

Many of the victims of these horrendous atrocities have the sweetest encounters with and intimacy with God. It is part of the healing process, but I believe it is also God taking special care for those who have been the most horrifically abused.

Sarah has come to experience God's love time and time again. He has learned to trust Him with her children. Jesus has come and spoken to her, revealed Himself to her and spoken words of healing to her heart. She no longer blames herself for all the problems in her life. She loves others well. She is serving God and others and raising her children to love and trust their Heavenly Father.

There are those who come to us who are so damaged and never do come to trust us or open up to God's perfect love. They are so hurt that they lash out and push everyone away. God always loves these hurting and abused children in powerful ways. Many times His love breaks through their doubt and distrust. Sadly, sometimes they run away in anger, believing we are going to betray them like everyone else.

I sincerely pray that we never lose one of the brokenhearted souls God sends our way.

THE SPIRIT OF THE LORD GOD

is upon me, because the LORD has

anointed me to bring good news to the

poor; he has sent me to bind up the

brokenhearted, to proclaim liberty to

the captives, and the opening of the

prison to those who are bound;

ISAIAH 61:1 (ESV)

Hannah's Story

Hannah's story is so unlike Sarah's story. Hannah didn't grow up in church. She also doesn't have her life together. During her lifetime, she's tried to commit suicide three times. She's been placed in various mental institutions on multiple occasions. She's struggled with drug, alcohol, and sexual addictions.

Even though Hannah is attractive, talented and has a high IQ, she struggles to keep a job. She also struggles to maintain any kind of relationships, whether romantic or friendship. She's even been homeless a few times in her life.

Hannah has several children that she hasn't seen in years. Her children are her greatest love, but she is filled with pain and shame as she tells why they were taken away from her. Her kids are in the care of family members who, on the outside, seem to have their lives more together than she does. These people who have custody of her kids are the same people who have abused her.

Hannah sees a psychiatrist and takes prescription drugs just so that she can cope with life. She has been approved by Medicaid for disability because of all her diagnoses. She hates her life and badly wants to be free, but she has no idea how to get there.

Her life has been a life from hell. Dying seems like the only known and sure way of escape. She was molested by her father at an early age. He taught her that God created her to serve men. This service to men includes taking care of their sexual fantasies. She was rewarded and punished for how well or poorly she performed. Her father sold her to other men and made money from the pornography that he created during these encounters. She was given drugs and alcohol to improve her performance and make her easier to control. She was also given drugs that were supposed to cause her never to remember what happened.

As a teen and later as an adult, she willingly prostituted herself to obtain the drugs she craved. This took her shame to another level. She assumed that it has always been her fault, and that something is wrong with her that caused her to do things that she knows are wrong.

On the surface, Hannah lived a normal life. She went to school, learned piano, took ballet, and even performed in her school's drama class. She looks beautiful and can sing well. You probably wouldn't suspect all the darkness under the veneer of normalcy.

Hannah has come close to getting the help she needs and craves numerous times.

Unbeknownst to her family, a friend brought her to OLF for ministry. She has a hatred that she doesn't understand toward church and Christians. She doesn't trust anyone. She even told us that she was sure that the friend who brought her to us had some ulterior motive. She accused us in our first session of being like all the other Christians - just in it for the money.

We listened patiently. She said that she didn't know why she told us as much about her life as she did. When we began to talk about Jesus, she cut us off and told us what she thought about Jesus and Christians. I love this part of ministry. When she was done, I agreed with her. You see, the Jesus that many people describe is not the Jesus I know and love. The Jesus I know and love doesn't need me to defend Him, and He is nothing like what many non-Christians describe. When I told her that I agreed with her, she seemed shocked and perplexed. I told her exactly why I wouldn't follow the Jesus she described either, with equal or greater feelings of disgust.

Then, I told her, as I have so many others, about the real Jesus. He is not religious. In fact, religious people hated Him, and He would intentionally do things to make them angry. I often see people get excited when I talk about the real Jesus, how He healed the sick, how demons hated Him and left when He commanded them to. I tell them how He allowed Himself to be beaten and crucified to heal broken hearts like theirs and how He does it even today because He rose from the dead.

You see, the Jesus that many people describe is not the Jesus I know and love. The Jesus I know and love doesn't need me to defend Him, and He is nothing like what many non-Christians describe.

Hannah is still trying to decide if she can trust us or this Jesus. But she is still coming back. She has sometimes stormed out and we haven't seen her for a while. She has accused us of many things at times. She one time sent another girl to our ministry whom she had met at an AA meeting. She had told this girl that she would feel loved here and that we had helped her a lot. That is the only way we have gotten to hear any compliment from her, but we will take it.

Hannah needs freedom. She needs Jesus. She needs to trust someone. God loves Hannah so much and speaks to her, calls her His beloved. He intercedes for her and weeps for her. He wants His church to know about her and to love her like He does.

Hannah at times wants to come to Freedom Park and live. At other times, she says she hates us. She is so afraid to trust anyone because it gives that person the ability to hurt her. She thinks that not trusting keeps her safe. She rejects everyone before they have a chance to reject her.

Let me be honest with you. Hannah is not one person. She is a conglomeration, a composite of very many of our clients. Every detail of her story could be told of the others we wrote about in this book and the many whose stories remain to be told.

Some of the Hannahs wouldn't care if we did tell their story and use their name. Others would likely try to sue us. Some do trust us enough to believe we are doing this because we care and want to help. Many others not only doubt our motives, in their minds they are certain everyone has an angle. They build their proof by judging every action. We will ask people to consider donating to help us save the Hannahs in this book. Some of the Hannahs will see us ask for money and will believe that we are using them to earn a profit. That is so far from the truth. We need funds because most of the Hannahs can't afford to pay anything for the ministry they so desperately need.

Pray for the Hannahs. Pray that they will come to know the real Jesus. Pray for them to find freedom from the torment in their minds, their hearts, their memories. Pray for them to get freedom from their addictions.

Pray for us as a ministry to be able to break through with all the Hannahs that God sends our way. We do have success with many, who like Hannah, start with a fear and/or distrust of Jesus and Christians and churches, and men, etc. They find His love, find community, and find freedom.

I am praying for an army of Hannahs to find freedom and to give the rest of their lives to the King of Kings, who loves them. I pray that these will become the front- line army in the war to rescue others out of slavery.

Would you join me in that prayer? While we wait for and watch the Lord build that army, would you prayerfully consider getting into the battle to free captives? It starts with your prayers but doesn't end there.

THE DISEASED HAVE YE NOT

strengthened, neither have ye healed that

which was sick, neither have ye bound up

[that which was] broken, neither have ye

brought again that which was driven away,

neither have ye sought that which was lost;

but with force and with cruelty

have ye ruled them.

EZEKIEL 34:4

Broken and Redeemed

When Martin arrived at OLF for ministry, it was a family member who brought him. The things he had been accused of were pretty serious. What greeted us was a highly intelligent and gifted man who had accolades from peers all around the country.

Martin was successful and especially gifted at what he did for a living. He had a beautiful wife and amazing children and grandchildren. He had been a leader in ministries and on boards of ministries and a significant donor to various ministries.

Martin's sister had sent him to us for ministry and even offered to pay for his ministry. Martin had been her spiritual hero and someone whom she had always looked up to until some things began to come to light. Now, she at least wanted him to get whatever help he needed.

Martin's wife had a lot to share with us. She told many stories of times that Martin would behave in ways that were totally uncharacteristic of anything she had seen or ever expected from him. She told of times when she tried to talk to Martin, but he acted like he didn't know her and wondered why she was calling him Martin. He gave her a different name. Later after these bizarre episodes that were almost always very hurtful, Martin would think that she was making up the whole story and lying to him about what had happened.

This made her hysterical at times. But as she committed to talking and trying to get to the bottom of things, the realization that she was telling the truth and the recollection of events would seep back into his consciousness. He would begin to weep over his actions and beg her for forgiveness.

Finally, Martin began to recover horrific memories of satanic rituals that he and other family members had been forced to endure. The afterschool childcare provided by a neighbor had not been the loving, caring place that he thought it had been. In fact, he wondered why a place that he had gone to for ten years of his life held almost no memories until now.

Memories of drugs, sexual abuse, pornography, and various kinds of mind control and programming came back, excruciating memory by memory. There were scars on his body that he had always wondered about until the memories came back of rituals where the wounds had occurred.

Martin had hidden the inner torture of his soul from everyone. He had found Jesus during college and found great freedom and joy and wanted to tell the world of the God whom he loved. That is what people knew about Martin. What drove him to serve and give was partially a mountain of guilt that would never go away.

The thoughts that plagued his mind of perverse things had covered him with shame and guilt throughout all these years. Why did he imagine doing things with men and children? He was a happily married man who loved his kids and grandkids. He was in every kind of Bible study, accountability group and men's ministry that he could find.

Martin had kept his addictions well-hidden and even mostly under control. He was admired for his zeal, his integrity, his commitment to friends, family and God. But deep within he feared the monster that he fought to contain and control. He thought that he was that monster.

Now that he had crossed some lines and given into the cravings of that monster, even many close friends considered him a monster. He had crossed the lines in mild ways compared to most people who have crossed those lines, but it didn't matter in the eyes of so many people in his life.

The secret was out. It was public. It had made a full page spread in the papers. He was too well known for it not to be spread to the world. His loving wife knew of the inner battle and knew that Martin was not a monster. This was not the man she loved and married. She held out hope that whatever this was, Martin could find freedom.

He was a happily married man who loved his kids and grandkids. He was in every kind of Bible study, accountability group and men's ministry that he could find.

God's grace is so incredible. One of the prayer ministers in the room had received healing from the same things Martin had been accused of and so had her kids. During the ministry session one of her kids messaged how God had really brought her healing to the point where she could face the man who had hurt her and love him. She read the email to Martin. It was a divine moment for sure.

There were a lot of tears shed as Martin was able to believe that God's love was for him as well. He was able to receive God's forgiveness and to forgive himself.

God began a beautiful and drawn-out process of helping Martin forgive the men and women who had been involved in his torture and torment.

He was even able to pray for God to set the people free who had been involved in his abuse.

The things that happened to Martin in his childhood, before he found Jesus were not an excuse for things that he did as an adult, but they sure helped him make sense of that monster. As Martin was able to connect with the memories and the broken pieces of his heart, he found greater ability to overcome the demons, the monster inside.

Martin has found such profound freedom. Many people still see him as a monster. They don't know his story. They have judged him as eternally unredeemable. That is so sad. He no longer has the dark thoughts or temptations. His wife no longer wonders who will be waiting for her when she gets home. She doesn't fret about which Martin might greet her, the angry one that calls itself Fred or the loving husband she married?

Most people think of women when they think of human trafficking and satanic rituals. The truth is some of the highest occult rituals involve males. There is no way to compare levels of abuse and rituals that people have been through, but the men do go through very unimaginable things to break them.

There seems to be a much greater stigma on the men and the types of abuse that they have endured as well. A man admitting he has been raped by other men seems to be so much harder of a subject for any man to ever talk about. For some reason the lie is that it negates a person's manhood to even admit what they have endured.

We see fewer men, though statistically the abuse is not as rare as one would think. The proportion of abused women willing to seek help is much higher than their male counterparts. I have prayed for a long time that God would give more and more men the grace to talk and deal with these issues and find healing. There is a great need in our nation for places for these men and boys to go for ministry and healing. Pray for the Martins in our world, and for all the men who have been victims and are too afraid to get the help they desperately need.

The most glorious aspect and privilege of ministering to the broken hearts whom God so loves is being part of their encounters with God. My best words and prayers are nothing compared to what God can say and do. I often feel like a witness to what God does. We have found that the most powerful healing happens when we facilitate an encounter with God and then we sit back and get a front row seat.

Sometimes God comes in a vision and snatches them out of their abuse and holds them and for that broken part, significant healing takes place. Or He comes like a lion and destroys the demons that have tormented them. He will take the little children to a beautiful field and play with them and dry their tears.

I cannot describe how incredible these encounters with God are, nor how healing they are for those who have been tormented for much of their lives. God is an amazing healer. He loves the brokenhearted, and he binds up their wounds.

FOR YE WERE AS SHEEP

going astray; but are now returned unto

the Shepherd and Bishop of your souls.

1 PETER 2: 25

John's Void

John came to us with a hunger and zeal like few his age display. He wanted to know more about God's power, how to heal the sick, how to set captives free, and all that Jesus did and does. He had not been out of high school for long but had already landed a high-paying job in his second career. Suffice it to say, John was an intelligent and highly motivated young man. He had bought his first house and seemed to have his life very much together.

John had grown up in a Christian homeschool family that went to church every week. Behind the beautiful facade was emotional, verbal, and spiritual abuse. Affairs by both parents caused John to battle rejection and the fear that he was destined for broken relationships. He was bullied in the church and homeschool groups, was often called gay, and had rebellion and stupidity spoken over him from a young age. He never found his place or fit in with any group. Instead, he turned his attention to living in online video-game fantasy worlds for most of his childhood, where he learned about magic, dragons, fairies, false gods, theft, murder, and alchemy.

He followed the pattern of his parent's, grandparent's, and great-grandparent's marriages in his dating relationships. He had cheated on girlfriends and felt a lot of guilt and shame. Most of his middle school and high school years he searched for relationships that either never happened or never brought fulfillment.

Around the age of twelve, a friend searched for the word 'sex' on his computer, and the world of porn was opened to him. The first time he searched for something at home, by himself, his father walked into the room, saw what he was doing, and stared blankly. His father had no idea how to handle the situation. He just turned and left the room. He never said a word to John about it or gave any correction. Sometime later his mom walked in on him. John said, "She went berserk." That only made John more curious and caused him to become better at hiding his new addiction.

Throughout high school his love for online video games transitioned to curiosity in the black hole of online pornography. Over the years, the addiction intensified, and what used to satisfy no longer brought the same pleasure. John began exploring every avenue of pornography. Nothing was too "out there." He eventually began experimenting on his own body and picked up an additional habit of overeating.

The "Christian" friends in his homeschool group, from all the really respected and good families, were experimenting with different drugs. John tried just about everything you can imagine. It started with liquor. Eventually that got boring until he added nicotine. He tried vaping for fun and then marijuana. As time went on in his dazed state of reality mixed with a constant feed of pornography, he found his way into LSD, mushrooms, DMT, coke, and meth. All while going to church as a completely different person, but showing up never fully present.

Eventually John experienced a devastating trail of events that started with moving to another city where he knew nobody. Then his heartbreak from an unhealthy attachment to a young woman was followed by his father's affair. All of this stacking up at once caused John to fall deeper into his addictions. The pornography, drugs, full on gluttony, and suicidal behavior intensified. All the pain, shame, hopelessness, and despair that he felt led him to seek out a prostitute. John eventually walked away from God and physically felt the pit in his stomach grow deeper.

God was speaking to John. He was calling John to return to Him. John had always had a zeal for God until he opened a spiritual doorway through prostitution. It was after opening that doorway that he had gone down the pathway of bondage, domination, sadism, masochism (BDSM). He began struggling with bisexuality, polygamy, and violent, lustful thoughts and acts. The spiral downward was quick, dark, and full of despair.

Eventually John experienced a devastating trail of events that started with moving to another city where he knew nobody. Then his heartbreak from an unhealthy attachment to a young woman was followed by his father's affair.

It eventually led John to damaging his body to the point of bleeding from his orifices as he couldn't find enough pleasure from the addictions. He became so desperate to stay high that he began digging through trash for leftover drugs and eventually started selling in large amounts so he could use them for his own escape.

John began to venture into New Age literature in a quest for spiritual understanding during this time as well. He read about astral projection, meditation, tarot card reading, clairvoyance, lucid dreaming, mind-reading, telepathy, UFOs, and more. At one time he believed he was talking to God for several days nonstop while on drugs.

John got piercings, satanic tattoos, shaved his head, and tried to change his name to Johnny. He wanted to shed the good boy and give himself over to become Johnny the bad boy.

When John came to us for ministry, he told us that John and Johnny were two different people. John was the person who loved and followed Jesus. John told us that he hated Johnny. He was the person who got high and did all the sinful, sexual stuff; he had a totally different personality.

I convinced John to let me talk to Johnny. He was very hesitant to let Johnny talk to me, but he did. Johnny had a lot of hurt and bitterness and tons of doubts and questions about God.

In one ministry session, Johnny had a powerful encounter with Jesus and repented of all his sin. John and Johnny have become one now, and John is experiencing so much more peace. He went home and experienced such a powerful breakthrough as he cried and allowed Jesus to comfort him.

John has spent quite a bit of energy telling people that he no longer wants to be called Johnny. That name represents a dark time in his life and he now is a new person.

One breakthrough led to another. John raced to church one Sunday morning and worshipped God with such abandon that in a single moment God took all eleven years of pornography, drug addiction, anger, hatred, gluttony, and shame away. And John never looked back.

The following week God grew John's left leg out to be the same length as his right leg, and healed his back pain. Shortly thereafter, God introduced John to fasting. He went on a nine-day fast and met Jesus face to face. John experienced such a heavy breakthrough later that night that he sobbed uncontrollably for half an hour as he experienced his deepest healing, and for the first time ever he truly believed he was loved.

John is walking with God. He has married a beautiful woman of God and is sold out to Jesus. His zeal and passion for the Lord are evident to all. He has learned to hear God's voice for real and wants to minister and serve others. God has used John to fill other starving Christians with Holy Spirit, free others from nicotine and alcohol addictions, and to simply care for the homeless by serving them on the weekends with his wife. His job and his finances are blessed, and he is debt-free. He has gained a joyful personality. He experiences real love and laughter instead of the counterfeit. The torment and rejection that ate away at his soul are gone. He has even picked up healthy eating and gardening. John wants everyone to experience the freedom and mercy God has given him.

There are a lot of other Johnny's out there. They were hurt and abused when they were young, and now they turn to alcohol, drugs, pornography and prostitutes to forget their pain if only for a moment. Just like Joy, they need to be set free from their prisons.

Johnny met Jesus and found true healing and freedom. And if we could reach all the Johns, there would no longer be such a demand for sex-trafficked girls.

EVEN AS THE SON OF MAN

came not to be ministered unto,

but to minister, and to give his

life a ransom for many.

MATTHEW 20:28

Joy Restored

How can we restore Joy? And Hannah, and Rosy, and Kelly and Sarah, and Martin and John?

The stories you have read would impact anyone. They impact us emotionally. I hope and pray that everyone who reads will have their eyes opened and will be inspired to respond generously and continuously. May you never forget what you have read. Too often we become aware of a need but without knowing what to do about the need, we never take action.

After reading these accounts, what should be the response? What can we do about all the tragedy and need? I hope that no one ignores this and treats it as just another story, a book to be read and forgotten.

I know there will be someone who reads this and even now, you are being abused and need freedom and healing. If you have been impacted by what you have read because you realize that you are a victim and you need freedom or healing, or restored joy, contact us at OLF and Freedom Park. We want to help you find freedom and joy.

For all the rest of you who have never experienced what you have read in these pages, or you now find yourself free from that world and want to help others, here are some responses that I hope this book invokes:

PRAY

First, PRAY, pray, pray! Pray for the multitudes of children today who are living in homes where they experience trauma and abuse on a daily basis. Pray for them to come to know that God really does love them and cares. Pray that they find freedom and healing, and faith in Jesus Christ.

Pray for those who are being abused inside the churches to be able to know that the real Jesus has nothing to do with their abuse. Pray that God will quickly expose the abusers and the abuse.

Pray for the 40 million girls and boys, women and men, who are right now trapped in slavery, being trafficked by family, boyfriends, judges, politicians, and celebrities. Pray for those who are being abused on a regular basis.

Pray that organizations and individuals who are abusing children will be exposed and dealt with appropriately. We need reform in our legal system, because many within that system are compromised or involved in these forms of abuse.

One thing that really needs serious prayer: There are many organizations that pose as organizations to help victims, when in reality they are places where victims find themselves right back in the world of Satanism, drugs, and even trafficking. We have found this all around the country. Organizations fund front organizations that look good on the outside, but victims from all around the country have told us that they had first-hand experience with organizations like that. Please pray that this type of activity is exposed and stopped. Ask for discernment for yourself regarding where to give and where to serve.

Please also pray for provision for Freedom Park and other organizations that are rescuing victims. These organizations need miraculous provision and lots of donations to accomplish this worthwhile goal, to provide love, care, and ministry as well as food, shelter and clothing for those coming out of bondage.

SERVE

Ministries like Operation Light Force and Freedom Park need all kinds of volunteer help. Everything from lawn maintenance and electrical to spending the night watching a house, to learning how to counsel the victims to anything else you can imagine.

Reach out and let us or another organization know that you want to serve in some capacity. If you have a professional skill and can donate your services, or if you just have free time and a willing heart, ask how you can help.

Your time, your talents and your life are valuable. You may not think that you have much to offer, but a heart willing to serve can do so much.

Counseling, Coaching, Mentoring

Here at OLF and Freedom Park we especially need people willing to be trained to counsel, coach, and mentor the people God sends to us. You could be a significant part of changing someone's life.

One thing that really needs serious prayer: There are many organizations that pose as organizations to help victims, when in reality they are places where victims find themselves right back in the world of Satanism, drugs, and even trafficking.

GIVE

The men and women, boys and girls who find themselves trapped and enslaved cannot afford to pay for their own freedom. We are talking physical freedom and spiritual freedom. The only way that this can be accomplished is through donations from people just like you.

OLF and Freedom Park need a house with some land that is away from everything. We are praying for at least $500,000.00 for our first rescue home. We have begun operating out of some fifth-wheel trailers but have come to realize that for us to house more people this is not an effective strategy. Those coming out of abuse, addictions, and bondage, need a lot of direct oversight and available help. The models that are working have larger homes where staff live and oversee 6-10 people at a time.

Someone might be able to give land. We also need vehicles. We need doctors, dentists, food, clothing. There are many things that need to be provided for.

The only way to meet the needs of these girls and boys, men and women is through the generous donations of people like yourself. We need monthly donors, grants, end of the year gifts of any amount. The cost to start up and run Freedom Park as we figured it will be $1,500,000.00. We are moving forward no matter what is given. But if everyone that we need to hire was hired and the buildings that we need are to be put in place, that is the amount we need. Our annual budget after startup will be half of that at $750,000.00. This is our faith and prayer target. Would you join us by praying and giving?

If not OLF and Freedom Park, would you please make a portion of your regular giving invested somewhere toward this very vital and worthy cause? The cause is on the heart of God. Has it hit your heart yet? Ask God what He would have you to give.

I believe God's vision for this need is much greater than what I have just shared. There is a need for homes for the boys and men who have been raped, abused, programmed and put through hell. There are men who were abused their entire childhood and now they battle with addictions, spousal abuse, sexual addictions. Some of these call us crying, begging to come and stay with us to receive ministry, have time and a place to heal, and just to be loved.

We need homes in every city of our nation. The crisis is everywhere, all around us. The need is great, and there are enough resources in God's kingdom. It is a costly ministry, but every single one of these people is worth it. They are worth the time. They are worth the gifts. They are worth the prayers and the tears.

Let's restore some Joy!

Bible Verses

FOR THE BROKEN SOUL

I have included throughout the book life-giving verses from the Bible that I believe speak directly to people who have been through severe trauma and had their souls shattered. I'm including those and others here so that you can experience the life-giving nutrition of God's Word. It is to nourish your spirit, soul and body. I would encourage you to read these and let them minister to you. I've also included a simple commentary with most of the verses to help you understand how it applies specifically to those with damaged hearts.

1 THESSALONIANS 5:23 (KJV) And the very God of peace sanctify you wholly; and I pray God your whole spirit and soul and body be preserved blameless unto the coming of our Lord Jesus Christ.

God is at work in each of our lives to sanctify us wholly. That mean completely, every part of our being. Our spirit needs to be whole, our soul needs to be whole, and our body needs to be whole. This is not automatic and instantaneous at salvation. This involves a journey of healing and transformation that is always progressing until we see Him face to face.

PSALM 34:18 (ESV) The LORD is near to the brokenhearted and saves the crushed in spirit.

The Lord is near to those who have been shattered. He saves those whose spirits have been crushed. He loves them. Will you?

PSALM 51:17 (ESV) The sacrifices of God are a broken spirit; a broken and contrite heart, O God, you will not despise.

A person's spirit can be broken as well as her heart. Although people often reject the broken ones, God never despises them. Ask God to help you love the brokenhearted as much as He does.

PSALM 69:20 (ESV) Reproaches have broken my heart, so that I am in despair.

One result of a broken heart is despair. One of the causes of a broken heart is reproach, which means being taunted, laughed at or made fun of. Have you ever been hurt by being laughed at?

PSALM 147:3 (ESV) He heals the brokenhearted and binds up their wounds.

The word for heals in this verse is rapha, which literally means to mend by stitching. The term binds up means to wrap up and hold firmly. Read the verse again, substituting "stitches" for heals and "wraps up and holds firmly" for binds. Pretty cool, isn't it?

ISAIAH 61:1 (ESV) The Spirit of the Lord GOD is upon me, because the LORD has anointed me to bring good news to the poor; he has sent me to bind up the brokenhearted, to proclaim liberty to the captives, and the opening of the prison to those who are bound.

These words were part of Jesus' mandate during His earthly ministry. And they are part of our mandate as well. Healing the brokenhearted is part of what it means to be like Jesus.

EZEKIEL 34:4 (KJV) The diseased have ye not strengthened, neither have ye healed that which was sick, neither have ye bound up that which was broken, neither have ye brought again that which was driven away, neither have ye sought that which was lost; but with force and with cruelty have ye ruled them.

> One of the signs of a false shepherd is his neglect or refusal to bind up the shattered. True shepherds/pastors bind up the brokenhearted and heal the sick.

EZEKIEL 34:16 I will seek that which was lost, and bring again that which was driven away, and will bind up that which was broken, and will strengthen that which was sick...

> God himself binds up the broken and strengthens the sick. He seeks them out. So should we.

LUKE 4:18 (KJV) The Spirit of the Lord is upon me, because he hath anointed me to preach the gospel to the poor; he hath sent me to heal the brokenhearted, to preach deliverance to the captives, and recovering of sight to the blind, to set at liberty them that are bruised...

> Jesus claims to have the calling of Messiah, which is to heal the brokenhearted.

PSALM 142:7 (KJV) Bring my soul out of prison, that I may praise thy name: the righteous shall compass me about; for thou shalt deal bountifully with me.

> A soul can be in prison/captive. When a person is set free from the prison where the soul has been held captive, praise comes easily.

JAMES 1:8 (ESV) He is a double-minded man, unstable in all his ways.

The Greek word here that is translated mind is actually the word for soul. A person's soul can be divided, and that causes a lot of instability in someone's life.

DEUTERONOMY 6:4-5 (KJV) Hear, O Israel: The LORD our God is one LORD: And thou shalt love the LORD thy God with all thine heart, and with all thy soul, and with all thy might.

If you are commanded to love God with all your heart and all your soul, then is it possible for part of your heart to love God while part of your heart fears Him, doubts Him, and does not love Him?

1 PETER 1:9 (KJV) Receiving the end of your faith, even the salvation of your souls.

The Greek word soteria is translated as salvation, but it also means health and healing, so this could read "the health of your soul." Now read it again.

1 PETER 2:25 (KJV) For ye were as sheep going astray; but are now returned unto the Shepherd and Bishop of your souls.

God is the shepherd, pastor, and bishop of our souls when we turn to Him.

PSALM 41:4 I said, LORD, be merciful unto me: heal my soul; for I have sinned against thee.

The soul can be in need of healing.

Heart and Soul

ISAIAH 53:11-12 (KJV) He shall see of the travail of his soul, and shall be satisfied: by his knowledge shall my righteous servant justify many; for he shall bear their iniquities. Therefore will I divide him a portion with the great, and he shall divide the spoil with the strong; because he hath poured out his soul unto death: and he was numbered with the transgressors; and he bare the sin of many, and made intercession for the transgressors.

Jesus' soul travailed, or was tormented, and was poured out in death. No one understands like Jesus does what it is like to be abused and traumatized. For Jesus it was by choice so He could heal and free us. What amazing love!

MATTHEW 20:28 (KJV) Even as the Son of man came not to be ministered unto, but to minister, and to give his life a ransom for many.

In this verse the word life is the word soul. In essence, one way of understanding this is that Jesus gave up His own soul to be punished, traumatized and to die, so that He could pay the ransom for others, for YOU, and for me.

LUKE 9:24,56 (KJV) For whosoever will save his life shall lose it: but whosoever will lose his life for my sake, the same shall save it. ... For the Son of man is not come to destroy men's lives, but to save [them]. And they went to another village.

The word save—sozo—means to make whole. The word used for life here is the same word for soul. When you substitute those words, the passage states that saving souls can very clearly mean healing broken hearts and souls.

JOHN 10:11, 15, 17 (KJV) I am the good shepherd: the good shepherd giveth his life [soul] for the sheep. ... As the Father knoweth me, even so know I the Father: and I lay down my life [soul] for the sheep. ...Therefore doth my Father love me, because I lay down my life[soul], that I might take it again.

Jesus is a shepherd for souls. As a good shepherd, Jesus laid down His soul for your soul, His life for your life. It was Father God's love for you that compelled Jesus to do this. Therefore, God the Father and Jesus have gone to great lengths to heal your broken soul.

JOHN 15:13 (KJV) Greater love hath no man than this, that a man lay down his life [soul] for his friends.

The greatest love of all? It is giving one's soul for a friend. Jesus showed the greatest love for you, and for me.

HEBREW 6:17-20 (NLT) God also bound himself with an oath, so that those who received the promise could be perfectly sure that he would never change his mind. So God has given both his promise and his oath. These two things are unchangeable because it is impossible for God to lie. Therefore, we who have fled to him for refuge can have great confidence as we hold to the hope that lies before us. This hope is a strong and trustworthy anchor for our souls. It leads us through the curtain into God's inner sanctuary. Jesus has already gone in there for us. He has become our eternal High Priest in the order of Melchizedek.

1 JOHN 3:16 (KJV) Hereby perceive we the love of God, because he laid down his life[soul] for us: and we ought to lay down our lives [souls] for the brethren.

God's very real love became tangible when Jesus gave his life for our lives. He laid down his soul for our souls.

HEBREWS 12:1-3 (NKJV) Therefore we also, since we are surrounded by so great a cloud of witnesses, let us lay aside every weight, and the sin which so easily ensnares us, and let us run with endurance the race that is set before us, looking unto Jesus, the author and finisher of our faith, who for the joy that was set before Him endured the cross, despising the shame, and has sat down at the right hand of the throne of God. For consider Him who endured such hostility from sinners against Himself, lest you become weary and discouraged in your souls.

Jesus had joy in His suffering and death because of how much He loved you. He was willing to go to any length to save you. What an encouraging thought.

ISAIAH 38:17 (KJV) Behold, for peace I had great bitterness: but thou hast in love to my soul delivered it from the pit of corruption: for thou hast cast all my sins behind thy back.

The forgiveness of sins brings healing to the soul. The guilt and shame regarding our sins brings a weight that many people cannot bear. The great news—and what brings us so much peace—is the reality that God forgives us and has removed the shame and guilt from us.

ISAIAH 61:10 (KJV) I will greatly rejoice in the LORD, my soul shall be joyful in my God; for he hath clothed me with the garments of salvation, he hath covered me with the robe of righteousness, as a bridegroom decketh himself with ornaments, and as a bride adorneth herself with her jewels.

The soul is joyful that is forgiven.

ISAIAH 58:10 (KJV) And if thou draw out thy soul to the hungry, and satisfy the afflicted soul; then shall thy light rise in obscurity, and thy darkness be as the noonday.

God will light your way if you care for afflicted souls.

Meet the Author

RICHARD MULL

Operation Light Force – Founder & President

Richard is the Founder and President of Operation Light Force (OLF), a ministry based near Tampa, FL, which he has headed up for over 22 years. OLF's vision is to equip men and women – old and young – to think, act and be like Jesus for their entire lives. As a renowned author, speaker and ministry leader, Richard Mull's books and ministry have been featured on JCTV, The 700 Club, CTN and Sky Angel. His 40-Day Revolution books have been featured at The Call events all around the world. He has also written *God Speaks Bible, Lord Disciple Me, The Jesus Training Manual,* and *Lord Heal Me.* A true servant of the God, he loves to listen to His Father's voice and is diligent to be about His business. Richard treasures moments with his amazing wife–Dawn and four children Andrew, Philip, Rachel and Nathanael (their "Miracle Boy"). Few things make him happier.

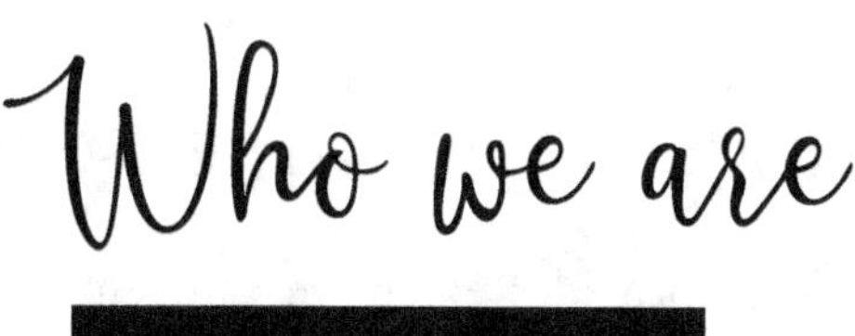

purpose

Think, act, and be like Jesus.

mission

To provide hurting people with love, compassion and prayer along with proven biblical methods to restore health to those in need of spiritual, physical, and emotional healing.

vision

OLF and Freedom Park strive to secure a house with land that is safe and secluded in 2022. We are praying for at least $500,000.00 for our first rescue home.

core values

LOVE: Everything we do must be grounded in and founded on the character of God Himself, that is rooted in love.

BIBLICAL TRUTH: Scripture is the foundation of all of our beliefs and practices in ministry.

JESUS CHRIST: Our model for ministry is Jesus and his disciples and apostles. The three primary facets of his model are: healing the sick, casting out evil spirits and preaching the good news of the Kingdom.

DISCIPLESHIP: Our primary objective is to train others up to walk in freedom, power, authority, and the three main facets which we call discipleship as Jesus did with His disciples.

HEALING: As disciples, we are called by God to minister healing to every form of sickness and infirmity and equip others to do so.

ABUNDANT LIFE: Christ came to bring us abundant life, and it is God's will for all men to experience the abundant life. Our call is to lead people into that.

DISCOVERY: As disciples, we are always to be learning, growing, and expanding in our understanding of the primary aspects of Jesus' model of discipleship.

HOPE/FAITH: Faith and hope are foundational to healing and wholeness in everyone's life. The basis of our faith and hope is God—His character and His Word.

12735 E. Wheeler Rd.
Dover, FL 33527

813.657.6147
operationlightforce.com

OPERATION LIGHT FORCE

Operation Light Force provides extensive care, nurture, ministry, and training to severely wounded people who have experienced trauma as a result of human trafficking, physical abuse, sexual abuse, emotional abuse, spiritual abuse, satanic ritual abuse, and PTSD. We walk alongside these over-comers and help them find healing, so that they and their families can live a life of freedom. People come from Tampa Bay, from other parts of Florida, other parts of the USA, and literally from all over the world.

We also minister to the needs of everyday families who are dealing with life's struggles: divorce, relationship issues, parenting, grief, marriage challenges, job loss and so much more. Life is full of hardships, struggles, and joys. We walk alongside people as they do life and support them as they face these challenges so that they can return to joy-filled living.

FREEDOM PARK

Freedom Park is more than a vision. It exists, but it needs a lot of help to not just survive, but thrive. We have had a growing number of opportunities to support people in similar ways, but have not had the resources to meet all of the needs brought to us. The testimony we have heard the most this year from those who have come to stay at Freedom Park is that the love that they have received is what has impacted them the most. God loves and cares for every one of these men and women. He wants His people to respond to this need with His love and His care. It is our sincere desire that we reflect His love as perfectly as possible and walk in His power to set people free and disciple them to serve and help others find freedom.